Connect
with
Text

What is Instructional Writing?

Charlotte Guillain

raintree
a Capstone company — publishers for children

Raintree is an imprint of Capstone Global Library Limited, a company incorporated in England and Wales having its registered office at 7 Pilgrim Street, London, EC4V 6LB – Registered company number: 6695582

www.raintree.co.uk
myorders@raintree.co.uk

Edited by Clare Lewis and Penny West
Designed by Philippa Jenkins and Tim Bond
Picture research by Gina Kammer
Originated by Capstone Global Library Ltd
Produced by Helen McCreath
Printed and bound by CTPS

ISBN 978 1 406 29686 0
19 18 17 16 15
10 9 8 7 6 5 4 3 2 1

British Library Cataloguing in Publication Data
A full catalogue record for this book is available from the British Library.

Acknowledgements
We would like to thank the following for permission to reproduce photographs:
Alamy: © Paul Matzner, 26; Capstone Studio: Karon Dubke, 12, 13, 16, 17, 21, 24, 25, 28, 29; Dreamstime: © Monkey Business Images, 5; Glow Images: Roberto Westbrook, 8; iStockphoto: alexsl, 14, IS_ImageSource, 7; Shutterstock: Daisy Daisy, 22, Feliks Kogan, 9, Forster Forest, 4, gpointstudio, 18, Ivan Dudarev, 19, Lakeview Images, 11, Mila May, 20, Monkey Business Images, 10, 27, Ruslan Guzov, 23; Wikimedia: The National Archives (United Kingdom)/Clive Uptton, 6

Disclaimer
All the internet addresses (URLs) given in this book were valid at the time of going to press. However, due to the dynamic nature of the internet, some addresses may have changed, or sites may have changed or ceased to exist since publication. While the author and publishers regret any inconvenience this may cause readers, no responsibility for any such changes can be accepted by either the author or the publishers.

Contents

Some words are shown in bold, **like this**. You can find out what they mean by looking in the glossary.

A world of non-fiction

When somebody mentions reading, do you immediately think about stories and comics? Or do you think of all the other types of reading you do every day? You probably read a lot of **non-fiction** every day without even realizing!

You read non-fiction to find out what is happening in the world.

Non-fiction is text that gives us different types of information. While **fiction** is stories and ideas that the writer makes up from his or her imagination, non-fiction is writing that is about real facts. We read non-fiction all the time for many different reasons. A non-fiction text could be a sign in the street, an information book in the library or the writing on food packaging! Newspapers, advertisements and information leaflets are all different types of non-fiction. This book is about a particular type of non-fiction called **instructional writing**.

Text around you

This book is a non-fiction text! What other non-fiction books have you read in your school or local library? You should be able to find information books to help you learn about many subjects and discover new interests.

What is instructional writing?

Instructional writing is a type of **non-fiction** that provides instructions, or guidelines. Instructions take the reader step by step through an activity that they haven't done before or can't remember. Instructions may include a few simple stages of the activity or be very detailed. They help the person reading the instructions to do something for him or herself and learn new skills and information safely.

Text in history

During World War II (1939–1945) there were many posters giving instructions to ordinary people. These helped them to save **resources** and stay safe. The instructions were short and clear so that people could see them as they passed in the street and remember the information. Do you see posters around you today? Are their messages short and clear, too?

HELP YOUR FUEL WATCHER

FUEL
HEAT·LIGHT·POWER
WATCHER

SHUT THAT DOOR!
HOLD THE HEAT–SAVE FUEL

SAVE FUEL
AT WORK

You use instructions in many different situations. When
you get a new toy or game and need to work out how to
build or play with it, you read the instructions. People
use instructions to make things, for example, a recipe
is instructions on how to cook food. Instructions can be
printed in books and on leaflets and you read them on
computer screens, too.

What are the features of instructional writing?

Most **instructional writing** includes the following features:

- Instructions often start by saying what the main goal of the task or activity is. For example, "This recipe makes 12 delicious banana muffins."

- There is usually a list of all the materials and equipment that the reader needs to complete the task. For example, "You will need a mixing bowl, a wooden spoon, 12 muffin cases and a baking tray."

You need to keep the recipe close by when you are cooking.

Text around you

In a public place, you will often find instructions telling you what to do in an emergency. These instructions need to be short and clear so people can read them quickly. They usually include pictures to help people understand what they need to do fast.

- Instructions show the reader how to finish the task properly and safely. The stages are introduced in the correct order and clearly explained.

- Instructions are usually written in a numbered or **bulleted list**. This helps the reader to follow each step in the correct order without getting muddled.

- Instructions often include **diagrams** to help explain what happens at each stage.

- You will often find extra advice or suggestions in instructions to help you finish the task successfully.

What sort of language is used in instructional writing?

It's important that instructions are simple, clear and direct. This helps the people reading the instructions to understand them fully and complete the task quickly and efficiently. Many of the sentences in instructions begin with **imperative verbs**, or "commands". For example, you might write "Turn the dial to the right" or "Whisk the eggs". "*Turn*" and "*Whisk*" are the imperative verbs, or commands. They clearly tell the reader how to complete the task.

You don't need to write a story when you're telling someone how to build furniture!

This sign needs very few words to warn the reader!

When you write instructions you may want to think about what the reader *shouldn't* do, too! Some of your sentences might begin with the word "Don't".

Text tips!

Instructions shouldn't include the language you might use if you were writing a story or a poem. You shouldn't use language such as **similes** or **metaphors** to add colour to the writing. You just need to tell the reader what to do as quickly and simply as you can. Most of the sentences in instructions are short. They only include **adjectives** or **adverbs** if they're really needed to help the reader understand what to do.

Who is the audience for the instructions?

All writers have to think about their reader and the **purpose** of their text when they write. Writers have to change their style for different readers. For example, you would write an email to your brother in a very different style to a letter to your teacher! When you write instructions you often don't know who will read them. This means it's a good idea to write them in a **formal** way. You want the reader to be able to complete the task or activity as easily as possible.

The instructions for a funny computer game are often written in a more chatty way, as if the writer is talking to the reader.

You can't assume the reader already knows something about the task. You will need to break the instructions down so that anyone can follow them.

When you write instructions for children, such as building a toy or following a recipe, you might want to write in a more **informal**, friendly tone.

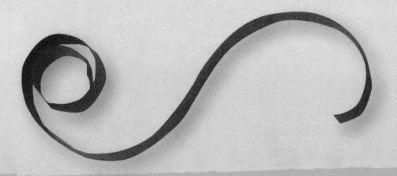

Pictures with instructions

Many instructions include photos or **diagrams**. This is because a picture helps the reader to better understand the written instructions. Some instructions are made up entirely of pictures, with no words! These instructions can be used by people in many different countries who don't speak the same language.

A map is a quick way of giving someone instructions for a route.

Text around you

Try making a model or following a recipe after you have covered up the pictures in the instructions. Were you able to do things properly just by reading the text? Was there any important information you missed by not seeing the pictures?

Recipes often include colour photographs of different stages. This helps the reader to make sure that they're doing things properly. It's much harder to know if you've stirred your mixture enough just by reading written instructions! When people write travel directions, they often include photographs of important places the reader will see on the route, or a map that gives visual instructions of the route. Some people find it easier to understand new information in pictures. Others find diagrams and photos help them to follow instructions faster.

Recipes

Recipes show us how to cook different types of food. Some cooks can make delicious meals from memory, but many people need instructions to guide them. Recipes for all sorts of different dishes are found in cookery books and on the internet.

It's important that recipes include clear lists of all the **ingredients** and tools, or utensils, needed. The reader will need to measure the ingredients carefully for the recipe to work, so this information must be accurate.

Recipes usually list the ingredients so the reader can check measurements carefully.

The photos included in recipes should look delicious so the reader will want to make the dish!

It's also important that the recipe tells the reader how hot their oven needs to be and how long they should cook their dish.

When people cook they use sharp utensils and hot ovens. Recipes need to have very clear safety instructions, especially when the readers are children.

Text tips!

If you write down a favourite recipe for a friend, you might like to include a serving tip. This could tell the reader what they might like to eat the dish with, such as serving garlic bread with pasta.

Travel directions

People often need directions if they're visiting a place for the first time. A **sat nav** in a car gives spoken instructions to help drivers reach their destination. Otherwise, people who are walking or driving somewhere unfamiliar often use written instructions to find their way.

City guidebooks often include instructions telling you how to get to interesting places.

If you're going for a walk in the countryside, written directions can help you to find your way.

Travel directions are usually in a numbered list, so the reader can follow the instructions in the correct order. The text gives details on how far to travel before any turn-offs. It might list significant buildings or **landmarks** the traveller should see on their journey. Written directions can point out things that a traveller may not see on a map, such as certain shops or a field of cows.

Text around you

If you're planning on visiting a museum or other public place, go to their website and click on the "How to find us" page. You'll often find written directions on how to reach the place, depending on how you are travelling. There's usually a map, too.

How to write instructions: Giving directions

Write some travel directions for a friend on how to get from school to your house.

1. Start by researching. Make notes on your way home from school. Are there any **landmarks** your friend should look out for? You could take photographs of buildings or other things you pass.

2. Start your instructions with a short **introduction**, saying what the directions aim to do.

3. Break down your directions into a numbered list. Make sure you don't miss out any important steps of the journey. Add how long each step should take.

4. Mention any points where the reader needs to be careful, for example, if they cross a busy road or walk next to a cycle path.

5. Write out or type up your directions and add any photographs you have taken.

6. Check your spelling and grammar. It's important that the reader understands your instructions clearly!

7. Draw a map if you think this will help the reader understand where to go.

8. Give the directions to a member of your family and walk with them as they follow your instructions. Can they find their way without any problems? Do you need to make any changes to your directions?

Instructions to make something

Many people read instructions to learn how to make things. New furniture often comes in **flat packs**. The buyer has to read the instructions and put it together themselves at home. If you've ever had a modelling kit you'll know how important it is to follow the instructions. If you miss out just one stage, it can be impossible to fix without starting all over again!

When you're gluing a model together, you have to do things in the right order – it can be very hard to unstick any mistakes!

Many instructions that tell people how to make things include **diagrams**. These are often numbered, like the text, so the reader knows what they need to do at each stage.

When you write instructions telling someone how to make something, make sure you include a list of tools and materials they'll need. Also, make sure you tell the reader how to put things together in the right order.

Write some instructions telling someone how to make something, such as a loom band bracelet.

1. Choose something you know how to make well. Think about all the different stages you go through to make it. Note them down in the correct order. Make sure you don't miss out any steps!

2. Start with a short **introduction**, saying what the reader will be able to do if they follow the directions.

3. Tell the reader what equipment and materials they need before they start.

4. Write your instructions clearly in a numbered list.

5. Think about whether you need to include any "Don't…" instructions. Are there common mistakes that you could warn the reader to avoid?

6. Point out safety issues, for example, are there any sharp tools?

7. Type up your instructions and add photographs you have taken of the different stages and the finished product.

8. Check your spelling and grammar are correct. Do all the instructions make sense?

9. Print off your instructions and draw **diagrams** you think will help the reader to understand.

10. Give your instructions to a friend and see if they can make the item you have described.

The rules of a game

Instructions are very important when you learn to play a new game. Whether it's a sport, a board game or a computer game, it's impossible to play properly without knowing the rules.

HOW TO PLAY
PÉTANQUE

The game is played by teams of one, two or three players on any small area of bare ground or crushed stone gravel, but never on grass or pavement.

A coin toss determines the first team to play. A player on the first team selects a starting place and draws a circle 14"- 20" in diameter on the ground. A player on the first team then tosses the jack a distance of 20' - 33'. The player's feet must remain within the circle until the ball touches the ground.

14"- 20"

20' - 33'

Gray team scores two points

Standing in the circle, a player on the first team then throws a ball to place it as close as possible to, but not beyond, the jack. The opposing team then throws its balls, attempting to get closer to the jack than the opponent. A team continues to throw until one of its balls is closer to the jack. Should the jack be hit, the game is played from the new location of the jack. In the event that the jack cannot be seen from the circle or is knocked out of bounds, the round is played over again.

When all the balls are thrown, the round is complete. The winning team is the one with the closest ball to the jack. They receive one ...... along with extra points for each ball nearer to the .... is

Text around you

These instructions for a simple ball game were put up in a park to show people how to play. Do you understand how to play this game? How do the **diagrams** help?

Often you get spoken instructions when you start a new sport. A coach or sports teacher tells you what to do as you try out the actions. However, it can still be useful to read instructions on how to play the sport afterwards. This helps you to remember the rules. Board games usually have numbered instructions that come in the box. These explain what all the equipment is for and how and when each player should take part. Computer games can be different, and often let you play straightaway. You can usually work out how the game works just by playing. However, many computer games provide instructions on the screen, which help you to improve as you play.

It's very hard to play a board game unless everyone understands the instructions!

Write some instructions on how to play a game.

1. Think about how the game works and make notes.

2. Start with a short **introduction**, saying how the game works. What is the player or team trying to do in order to win?

3. How many people do you need to play the game and what equipment do you need?

4. Write instructions on how to play the game in a numbered or **bulleted list**. Do things have to happen in a particular order?

5. Do you need to include any "Don't..." instructions? How might players break the rules?

6. Warn the reader if they need to be careful playing the game, so that nobody gets hurt.

7. Type up your instructions. Add any photographs you have of people playing the game.

8. Check and edit your instructions. Do they make sense? Are they simple and clear to understand?

9. Print off your instructions and draw any **diagrams** you think will help the reader to understand how to play the game.

10. Give your instructions to a friend and see if they can play the game without any problems. Do you need to add any more instructions?

Glossary

adjective word that describes a noun

adverb word that describes a verb

bulleted list list of items presented with bullet points

diagram picture that shows how something works or how to do something

fiction story that has been made up

flat pack usually furniture that is sold in pieces in a flat box. The buyer then puts the furniture together at home.

formal following the expected rules

imperative verb word that commands, or tells, someone what to do

informal relaxed and not following all the rules

ingredient one of the foods needed for a recipe

instructional writing writing that tells people what to do

introduction beginning of a piece of writing that explains what topic the writing will cover

landmark thing that can easily be seen in the open air

metaphor when something is described as being another thing

non-fiction writing about real-life facts

purpose plan or aim

resource something that can be used

sat nav device that tells you where to go using satellites

simile when one thing is compared to another

Find out more

To learn more about instructional writing and how to do it well, take a look at the following books. Use the websites listed below and the "How to" topics in this book to test out your new instructional writing skills!

Books

Instruction Texts for Ages 7–9 (Writing Guides), Leonie Bennett (Scholastic, 2009)

Making Better Sentences: The Power of Structure and Meaning (Find Your Way with Words), Liz Miles (Raintree, 2014)

Organizing and Using Information (Information Literacy Skills), Beth A. Pulver (Heinemann Library, 2009)

The Structure of Words: Understanding Roots and Smaller Parts of Words (Find Your Way with Words), Rebecca Vickers (Raintree, 2014)

Websites
www.bbc.co.uk/bitesize/ks2/english/writing/instructions/read/1
Find out more about writing instructions on this BBC website.

cache.lego.com/bigdownloads/buildinginstructions/4115753.pdf
Look at these diagrams on the Lego website, telling you how to build a model of a hang glider. Try to write the instructions using words. Why do the diagrams work better?

www.crickweb.co.uk/ks2literacy.html#teaseq
Click on "Instruction sequencer" on this website and try putting the instructions in the correct sequence.

Index